PHILADELPH
THE CITY AT A GLANCE

Wells Fargo Building
This 1928 H-shaped high-rise, designed by
architects Simon & Simon, features stonework
by the Piccirilli Brothers. It was remodelled
by local firm Cope Linder in 1996.
123-151 S Broad Street

Wanamaker Building
Pioneering department store Wanamaker's
may be long gone, but Daniel Burnham's
palatial granite building, which opened in
1910, is a reminder of its golden age.
1300 Market Street

One Liberty Place
The stepped spire of Helmut Jahn's Chrysler-
esque skyscraper, completed in 1987, singles
it out on the skyline. Two Liberty Place next
door was also design^...... ....
1650 Market Street

GW00686272

City Hall
A massive structure
build, this is the geo
centre of Philadelph
of its founder, Willia
the top for a stunni
See p013

Comcast Center
Robert AM Stern's understated sliver of glass
is the tallest tower in the city.
See p012

Inquirer Building
Rankin, Kellogg and Crane's iconic Beaux Arts
building housed *The Philadelphia Inquirer*
from 1925 until 2012. It is a counterpoint to
City Hall, located six blocks to the south.
400 N Broad Street

INTRODUCTION

THE CHANGING FACE OF THE URBAN SCENE

Philadelphia has, at various points in its history, been one of the world's great cities – the centre of cultural and political activity in colonial America; the first capital of the United States; and the young nation's first industrial giant. But it's just 130km south-west of New York, and in the national perception it regularly seems to take a back seat to the Big Apple. In 2005, *The New York Times* called it 'the next borough', a nickname that outraged many locals. And with good reason. Philadelphia is a sophisticated, vibrant city that is once again coming into its own, thanks largely to a young, diverse population determined to carve out a metropolis that is eminently liveable and refreshingly unpretentious.

That said, you will not get a taste of the best parts of Philly if you stay on the tourist track. Instead, explore its neighbourhoods. Whether historic (Old City) or up-and-coming (Kensington and adjacent Fishtown), they are all distinctive and easily accessible, and peppered with many excellent restaurants and one-off shops. And Philadelphians are affable, savvy urbanites. Their quirky, self-effacing attitude is part of what makes this place so alluring.

Combine its urban and architectural attractions with the charm of the surrounding Pennsylvania countryside, and you certainly won't be stuck for things to do here, or be hankering to hotfoot it to NYC or Washington. But don't try to fit everything in. Take our word for it, this is a destination that you'll want to revisit.

ESSENTIAL INFO
FACTS, FIGURES AND USEFUL ADDRESSES

TOURIST OFFICE
Independence Visitor Center
1 N Independence Mall West
T 800 537 7676
www.discoverphl.com

TRANSPORT
Airport transfer to Center City
Airport Line trains depart Philadelphia
International Airport every 30 minutes
from 5am to midnight. The journey takes
25 minutes
Car hire
Avis
Philadelphia International Airport
T 215 492 0900
Public transport
The subway runs Sunday to Thursday, 5am
to midnight; Friday to Saturday, 24 hours.
Night Owl buses operate in-between. The
Phlash bus stops at 22 key locations every
15 minutes from 10am to 6pm
www.septa.org
Taxis
PHL Taxi
T 215 232 2000
Cabs can also be hailed on the street

EMERGENCY SERVICES
Emergencies
T 911
24-hour pharmacy
CVS
1826 Chestnut Street
T 215 972 0909
cvs.com

CONSULATE
British Honorary Consulate
33rd floor, 1818 Market Street
T 215 557 7665
ukinusa.fco.gov.uk

POSTAL SERVICES
Post office
3000 Chestnut Street
T 215 895 9012
Shipping
UPS
1229 Chestnut Street
T 215 568 4555

BOOKS
Forty Years at the Institute of
Contemporary Art by Johanna
Plummer (Institute of Contemporary Art)
Louis I Kahn by Robert McCarter
(Phaidon Press)
Philadelphia Architecture: A Guide
to the City by John Andrew Gallery
(Paul Dry Books)
Searching for Philadelphia by
David S Traub (Camino Books)

WEBSITES
Architecture
www.philadelphiacfa.org
Arts
www.icaphila.org
Newspapers
www.philadelphiaweekly.com
www.philly.com

COST OF LIVING
Taxi from Philadelphia International
Airport to city centre
$28.50
Cappuccino
$3.50
Packet of cigarettes
$6
Daily newspaper
$1
Bottle of champagne
$90

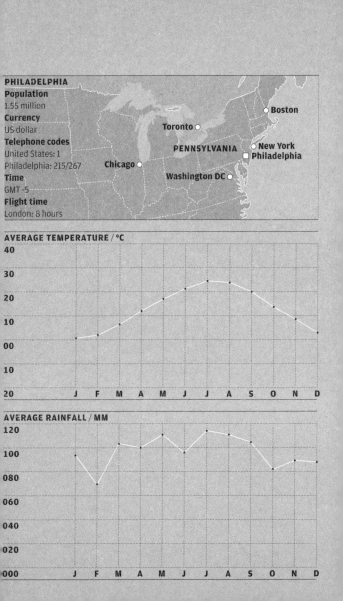

PHILADELPHIA
Population
1.55 million
Currency
US dollar
Telephone codes
United States: 1
Philadelphia: 215/267
Time
GMT -5
Flight time
London: 8 hours

Boston

Toronto

PENNSYLVANIA

New York
Philadelphia

Chicago

Washington DC

AVERAGE TEMPERATURE / °C

40												
30												
20												
10												
00												
10												
20	J	F	M	A	M	J	J	A	S	O	N	D

AVERAGE RAINFALL / MM

120												
100												
080												
060												
040												
020												
000	J	F	M	A	M	J	J	A	S	O	N	D

NEIGHBOURHOODS

THE AREAS YOU NEED TO KNOW AND WHY

To help you navigate the city, we've chosen the most interesting districts (see below and the map inside the back cover) and colour-coded our featured venues, according to their location; those venues that are outside these areas are not coloured.

UNIVERSITY CITY

Six colleges and universities are situated here so, as you'd expect, this is a district with a lively going-out and arts culture. Don't miss the ICA (see p026), the White Dog Cafe (3420 Sandom Street, T 215 386 9224) and hip concert venue The Rotunda (4014 Walnut Street, T 215 573 3234).

SOUTH PHILADELPHIA

South Philly is largely residential, though it gets attention for South Street's nightlife, Fabric Row on S 4th Street and the Italian Market – Isgro Pasticceria (see p032), in particular, is popular for its baked goods. You will also find myriad Asian and Latino businesses, and chic Serpico (see p039).

FAIRMOUNT/ART MUSEUM

Most people know this neighbourhood for the Philadelphia Museum of Art (see p014) and Fairmount Park, which begins here. Its quiet streets are a draw too, as are tours of the giant 1829 Eastern State Penitentiary (2027 Fairmount Avenue, T 215 236 3300). To the west, Kelly Drive offers fantastic city and river views; it's also great for jogging.

WASHINGTON SQUARE WEST

The area between Society Hill and the tony Rittenhouse Square languished for years as urban rejuvenation swirled around it. Gentrification here is catching up, but for now the area still mixes hipness and grit. Check out its restaurants and bars, such as Vedge (see p038) and Mercato (see p046).

OLD CITY

The oldest part of Philadelphia, along the Delaware waterfront, has been reborn as a district of lofts, restaurants and smart shops at its northern end, while there are stately row houses in Society Hill to the south. Independence Mall can be choked with tourists but quiet corners do exist.

CENTER CITY NORTH

Business is the focus of the area north of Market Street. But there is fun to be had; seek out Reading Terminal Market (51 N 12th Street, T 215 922 2317) for top local produce and Amish specialities, the PSFS Building (see p082) and the Pennsylvania Academy of the Fine Arts (see p064).

RITTENHOUSE SQUARE

Once the enclave of Philadelphia's elite, this area remains one of the best bets for shopping and dining, especially on Walnut Street. There are office towers to the north and east, but the south is still crisscrossed by attractive low-level streets. Pub & Kitchen (see p041), one of our favourite Philly eateries, is here.

NORTHERN LIBERTIES

Located just outside Philadelphia's original boundaries, this area got its name because William Penn gave anyone who bought land in the city a free plot here. Today, a young crowd, who favour fashionable Fishtown venues such as Jerry's Bar (see p032), are filling up its townhouses and factories.

LANDMARKS
THE SHAPE OF THE CITY SKYLINE

When William Penn founded Philadelphia, he envisioned a city of townhouses ringed by large country estates. The colonists who developed it had other ideas. Dividing and subdividing Penn's lots, they formed a dense urban zone that eventually spilled out miles throughout the Delaware valley. Modern Philly's sprawl of suburbs, malls and freeways may seem as inscrutable as any metropolitan jumble, but at its core it's a superb piece of urban planning.

Credit for the layout of Center City must go to Penn. His 1682 grid plan – the first of its kind in the US – stands today. Its focal point, literally and symbolically, is City Hall (see p013); its clock tower defined the skyline for decades, though it has since been eclipsed by a host of skyscrapers, including the Comcast Center (see p012). Philadelphia's colonial beginnings can be seen in Old City, which is anchored by Independence Hall (520 Chestnut Street, T 215 965 2305), one of the finest Georgian buildings in the US.

Today, Philly is not only shooting upwards, but also dealing with past missteps on the ground, such as the no-man's-land along the Delaware waterfront. Isolated when Interstate 95 cut through in the 1960s, it is now being reborn as a series of parks and mixed-use projects. Hopefully, future developments will maintain the juxtapositions of style and scale that give the cityscape its unique appeal: by turns gritty and polished, but always interesting.

For full addresses, see Resources.

Cira Centre

Cesar Pelli designed this office block to be a new landmark on the west bank of the Schuylkill, a counterpoint to the towers of Center City across the river and the classical lines of 30th Street Station (see p086) just to the south. Though taller buildings have risen nearby since it was completed in 2005, Cira Centre is still a standout. Pelli gave the 133m structure a faceted profile, and clad it with blue glass that gleams like quartz crystal in certain lights. At night, a grid of colour-shifting LEDs built into the curtain wall accent its profile. Unfortunately, the site that helps make Cira Centre so dramatic (it perches on a platform beside a vast railway yard) also means that it lacks spark at street level; plans to invigorate the surrounding area stalled along with the economy.
2929 Arch Street, www.ciracentre.com

Comcast Center

Standing beneath this dazzling triumph, you feel every bit of its imposing 297m height. And yet the HQ of the largest cable company in the US, designed by New York-based architects Robert AM Stern, is so reflective, its tapered form so simple, that it slips very quietly into the skyline. This is in part due to the sheer glass skin (the original plan proposed a Kasota stone facing), as well as pleated corners and a transparent crown. Stern's design really excels at street level, where an expansive public plaza leads to a 33.5m-high lobby with a winter garden and a 185 sq m HD video screen, The Comcast Experience, which was designed by the Niles Creative Group. Myriad eco features make this one of the tallest green buildings in the States.
1701 John F Kennedy Boulevard,
T 800 934 6489

City Hall

When the ground was broken for City Hall in 1871, architects John McArthur Jr and Thomas U Walter intended for it to be the world's tallest structure. By the time construction was completed in 1901, the 167m tower had been eclipsed in height, and their fussy Second Empire style was thoroughly outdated. Fortunately, this handsome building has survived various redevelopment schemes and remains an arresting and much-loved symbol of proud Victorian Philadelphia. Don't miss the 250 or so sculptures carved by Alexander Milne Calder, especially the 11.3m-high bronze statue of William Penn that tops them all. You can't just wander in, but guided tours, which take two hours and include access to the observation deck, run on weekdays.
Broad Street/Market Street,
T 215 686 2840

Philadelphia Museum of Art

Probably best known for its front steps, which appeared in the Rocky films, the 1928 Museum of Art bookmarks the north end of the Benjamin Franklin Parkway. Architect Horace Trumbauer, working with Zantzinger, Borie and Medary, wrapped the building – a museum as temple – in golden Minnesota limestone, limiting exterior ornamentation to bronze griffins at the roofline and Carl Paul Jennewein's polychrome figures in the northern wing's tympanum. Inside is a vast collection of international art and artefacts; we suggest concentrating on the American galleries, as well as the textile exhibits of the nearby Perelman Building (2525 Pennsylvania Avenue), an art deco monument restored in 2007 by architects Gluckman Mayner. *2600 Benjamin Franklin Parkway, T 215 763 8100, www.philamuseum.org*

HOTELS

WHERE TO STAY AND WHICH ROOMS TO BOOK

Philadelphia's hotels have long been geared towards two crowds: business travellers and package holidayers. Lucrative as that may have been, it left the city with a glut of bland chains and budget options with not much in-between, except the odd chintzy B&B. In recent years, however, things have taken a turn for the better.

Center City is the heart of hotel land, and is the best place to stay for exploring major attractions. Elegant The Ritz-Carlton (10 S Broad Street, T 215 523 8000), housed in McKim, Mead & White's early 20th-century bank building, and the Loews (see p023) are sure bets, as is Le Méridien (see p018). A pair of Kimpton properties, the Palomar (opposite) and the Monaco (433 Chestnut Street, T 215 925 2111), have brought the group's signature plush, contemporary style to the city, and a new breed of apartment hotels, including Roost Midtown (see p020) and the AKA Rittenhouse Square (see p022), offer stylish suites large enough to host your entourage. The sleek, fully refurbished The Logan (1 Logan Square, T 215 963 1500) has a prime location on the Benjamin Franklin Parkway.

Meanwhile, the Four Seasons will occupy the upper floors of a newly built 342m tower near the Comcast Center (see p012) from 2017, and a long-awaited W hotel is set to open in 2018 close to The Ritz-Carlton. The SLS group has also announced plans for a 2017 Kohn Pedersen Fox-designed property in Center City. *For full addresses and room rates, see Resources.*

Hotel Palomar

Situated in a restored 1929 high-rise off Rittenhouse Square, the Palomar injects a much-needed dosage of contemporary design into the Philadelphia scene. The interiors, by LA-based Powerstrip Studio, feature deco-inspired elements, including a marble fireplace in the lobby and angular lamps and headboards in the 230 rooms. The sprawling Presidential Suite (above) has superlative city views, a parlour with a six-seater dining table, a lounge, and a bathroom with a Fuji spa tub. The on-site restaurant and bar, Square 1682 (T 215 563 5008), serves top seasonal cocktails. Try the Wildwood Ave & Boardwalk, a mix of Bulleit bourbon, Luxardo maraschino, Ramazzotti bitters and local Root liquor (see p093), or a classic whisky Sazerac. *117 S 17th Street, T 215 563 5006, www.hotelpalomar-philadelphia.com*

Le Méridien

It is hard to believe that this dignified 1907 Georgian building was a YMCA for nearly a century, before the 2010 Le Méridien conversion classed things up. The 202 rooms, by designers Forchielli Glynn, are minimalist but comfortable. Some run on the small side; we suggest booking a south-facing Suite (pictured) for more elbow room and a city view.
1421 Arch Street, T 215 422 8200

Roost Midtown

Roost redefined extended-stay hotels when it opened in 2014. Its 27 spacious studios, and one- and two-bedroom apartments, each with kitchens and laundry utilities, are tucked across two floors of a 1920s residential building. Surprising perks include Geneva sound systems, Apple TVs, Bonavita coffee-makers, Davines toiletries and Sferra linens. New York-based firm Morris Adjmi is responsible for the interiors, which match antique Turkmen rugs with midcentury-inspired furniture and original art from LUMAS, all spot on for Roost's vibe of effortless cool. Also on the amenity list are a bike-sharing scheme, a library and free entrance to a close-by fitness club, in addition to a concierge service. The hotel welcomes short-term stays too if rooms are free.
111 S 15th Street, T 267 737 9000, www.myroost.com/midtown

AKA Rittenhouse Square

With its understated entrance and stately Beaux Arts facade, the AKA, which opened in 2007, is easy to mistake for a residential building. There's good reason: the rooms were carved out of a 1914 apartment block, and the hotel has maintained a low-key neighbourhood feel. The suites range from studios to two bedrooms, and each has a marble bathroom, a kitchen and modern furnishings that complement original fireplaces and plasterwork. Our favourites are on the south-west corner, overlooking Rittenhouse Square. There is no pool and only a small gym, but guests are granted access to the Sporting Club at The Bellevue. Do pay a visit to the stylish a.kitchen (T 215 825 7030) and adjacent a.bar (T 215 825 7035), which are both popular with locals. *135 S 18th Street, T 215 825 7000, www.stayaka.com*

Loews

Set in the PSFS Building (see p082), one of America's finest modernist skyscrapers, this hotel has serious design pedigree. An overhaul in 2000 kept the sophisticated public spaces and turned the former office floors into 581 rooms and suites, which were updated in 2014 by Daroff Design using a monochrome palette shot through with primary colours. Though the scheme errs on stark, the rooms are comfortable and spacious, and those on higher floors have great views; a west-facing Luxury King offers a panorama of the city skyline. There is also a 20m lap pool (above) and spa. Deals are best sealed in the hotel's 33rd-floor conference rooms; the exquisite art deco setting was once reserved for the highest echelon of Philadelphia business. *1200 Market Street, T 215 627 1200, www.loewshotels.com*

24 HOURS

SEE THE BEST OF THE CITY IN JUST ONE DAY

Most visitors to Philadelphia make a beeline for Independence Mall to see the greatest hits of colonial America. There's nothing wrong with that, but we'd rather show you a different side of the city: fine neighbourhood restaurants and bars, contemporary art and new architecture. The centre is compact enough to explore on foot, or hire wheels at an Indego bicycle station (www.rideindego.com).

Start with a meander around Society Hill – stomping ground of the 18th-century elite – exploring the neighbourhood's lanes for an excellent introduction to Philly's urban diversity. Close by are the shops and eateries of happening Midtown Village; look for design-forward homewares at Open House (107 S 13th Street, T 215 922 1415) before a mod Mediterranean lunch at Barbuzzo (110 S 13th Street, T 215 546 9300). Paul Philippe Cret's elegant landscaping is an ideal setting for people-watching in Rittenhouse Square, best followed by a tipple at a.bar (see p022). Devote the rest of the day to the American masters at the Barnes Foundation (see p073).

In the evening, make the trip north to hip Fishtown. We suggest dinner at Kensington Quarters (see p044) or in the laidback beer garden of Frankford Hall (1210 Frankford Avenue, T 215 634 3338). Round out the night with a punch bowl in the somewhat over-the-top Emmanuelle (1052 N Hancock Street, T 267 639 2470) lounge, or fantastic cocktails in the subterranean Franklin Bar (see p030). *For full addresses, see Resources.*

09.30 Fairmount Park

There are scores of excellent works on display around the city, thanks in large part to the Association for Public Art, a private group established in 1872. It's responsible for commissioning some of Philadelphia's most cherished pieces; Antoine-Louis Barye's *Lion Crushing a Serpent* in Rittenhouse Square heads a long list. Many can be viewed on a stroll through Fairmount Park, which stretches north-west from the Philadelphia Museum of Art (see p014). It is home to classic as well as contemporary sculptures, such as Mark di Suvero's *Iroquois* (above), which is named after a Native American Indian tribe and fashioned from I-beams; Roxy Paine's *Symbiosis,* in stainless steel; and Robert Morris' weathered *The Wedges*. Find audio guides and a map on the APA website. *www.associationforpublicart.org*

11.00 Institute of Contemporary Art
Pay attention to the work displayed at
Philly's ICA. Since it was founded in 1963,
the museum has had a knack for catching
artists on their way up. It featured Agnes
Martin, Cy Twombly, Robert Mapplethorpe
and Andy Warhol, among others, before
they became superstars. The museum
itself, housed in a 1991 building designed
by Adèle Naudé Santos within the grounds
of the University of Pennsylvania, mounts
exhibitions in all disciplines and hosts a full
roster of events, including film screenings,
performance art, lectures and workshops.
The 2015 Barbara Kasten retrospective,
'Stages' (right), displayed five decades of
work by the multimedia artist, including
a site-specific video projection. ICA has a
fantastic publishing programme too.
118 S 36th Street, T 215 898 7108,
www.icaphila.org

14.30 Art in the Age

Steven Grasse launched his brand Art in the Age of Mechanical Reproduction (the name is taken from Walter Benjamin's 1936 essay) in 2006 with a line of artist-designed T-shirts. Two years later, he opened this Old City storefront, filling it with an eclectic selection of products: Nipomo blankets, Juniper Ridge cologne, Otter-Messer pocket knives, Teranishi leather goods and clothing from labels such as Penfield, Fidelity Sportswear and Gitman. You can also try Art in the Age's craft liquor (see p093). Local firm Rissay conceived the rustic-chic space, which is all about exposed brick and a 19th-century apothecary cabinet. This is your perfect introduction to the independent boutiques that pepper the neighbourhood.
116 N 3rd Street, T 215 922 2600, www.artintheage.com

17.00 The Rittenhouse Spa & Club

This luxe spa and salon in The Rittenhouse hotel (T 215 546 9000) established a new standard when it surfaced from a sizeable reimagining by BLT architects in 2014. The Paul Labrecque salon features a traditional barbershop (above), and spa areas sport a minimal style, with a subdued ambience and plenty of wood and stone. Treatments include the Detox Marine Algae Wrap, for $140, which wards off toxins, and the Citrus Drench, $130, an hour-long body scrub and massage using Natura Bissé products. The Gentleman's Ultimate Treatment Experience, $475, includes hand and foot grooming, back exfoliation and a glass of top-notch Scotch – add a classic wet shave to complete the indulgence. There is also a sauna, steam room and indoor pool.
210 W Rittenhouse Square, T 215 790 2500, www.therittenhousespaclub.com

20.00 The Franklin Bar

This is a smart spot where cocktails are king. The drinks list gives modern twists to classic tipples, and purveys seasonal quaffs designed around cute concepts; past libations have conjured up summers at the New Jersey shore. One floor above is The Upstairs Bar, Franklin's version of a Philadelphia dive, which specialises in 'citywides' — a beer and spirit chaser. *112 S 18th Street, T 267 467 3277*

URBAN LIFE
CAFÉS, RESTAURANTS, BARS AND NIGHTCLUBS

Eating out in Philadelphia has long been a wonderful thing, only inflated by a fresh crop of chefs. Michael Solomonov's restaurants are surely some of the best in town, with Abe Fisher and Dizengoff (opposite) being the perfect introduction. In Old City, High Street on Market (see p050) and adjacent Fork (306 Market Street, T 215 625 9425) showcase Eli Kulp's inventive yet classic North American menus, and Kensington Quarters (see p044) promotes organic, whole-animal cooking in Fishtown. Still leading the charge are Stephen Starr, who is responsible for splashy steakhouse Barclay Prime (see p042) and the farm-to-table Talula's Garden (210 W Washington Square, T 215 592 7787), and his alumnus Jose Garces, who heads up the casual taco joint Buena Onda (see p037).

The city takes its sandwich shops just as seriously as its fine-diners; we'll happily queue for local speciality, the cheesesteak, at John's Roast Pork (14 E Snyder Avenue, T 215 463 1951), or cannoli at Isgro Pasticceria bakery (1009 Christian Street, T 215 923 3092).

Philly's nightlife remains rough around the edges. We favour spots where substance trumps attitude: Jerry's Bar (129 W Laurel Street, T 267 273 1632) is a polished gastropub with skilfully made cocktails, easy-to-miss Hop Sing Laundromat (1029 Race Street) has an impressive list of spirits, and the dive bar Johnny Brenda's (1201 N Frankford Avenue, T 215 739 9684) is best for live music. *For full addresses, see Resources.*

Abe Fisher and Dizengoff

Restaurateurs Steve Cook and Michael Solomonov have long been Philadelphia favourites for their chic Israeli restaurant Zahav (T 215 625 8800), so there was a real clamour when they opened this twin-concept spot in 2014. The innovative daily varieties of hummus are the main draw at lunch-only Dizengoff (overleaf), while chef Yehuda Sichel puts a modern spin on traditional Jewish recipes at Abe Fisher (above). You can't go wrong with either. Dizengoff chef Emily Seaman partners with local farms to source ingredients for her chickpea-based dips, and when Sichel isn't turning staples such as chopped liver and schnitzel on their heads, he's cooking pastrami-smoked Montreal short ribs – a dish that already has cult status.

1623-5 Sansom Street, T 215 867 0088,
www.abefisherphilly.com

Buena Onda

Chef Jose Garces has built a restaurant empire in Philly, dishing out everything from Spanish tapas at Amada (T 215 625 2450), which remains at the top of the small-plate game, to the refined cuisine of Mexican City at cheeky Distrito (T 215 222 1657). Launched in 2015, Buena Onda has a menu that is structured around Garces' famous fish tacos – varieties include the catch of the day, shrimp and mahimahi,

as well as chicken, pork and beef options. Order with an accompaniment of nachos, guacamole or *esquites*, a Mexican corn salad, and a K38 Pale Ale by local brewer Yards (T 215 634 2600). DC-based CORE's fresh interior of beachy blues and slatted lightwood cladding perfectly complements the tasty, no-fuss dishes here.
1901 Callowhill Street, T 215 302 3530,
www.buenaondatacos.com

Vedge

Stylish and inventive, Vedge has secured a raft of acclaim since opening in 2011, all without serving any meat – still fairly uncharted waters for upscale American restaurants. Husband and wife Richard Landau and Kate Jacoby head the kitchen here, turning out dishes such as terrine of salt-roasted yellow beet; spicy tofu, capers, red onion and cucumber; and grilled seitan served with smoked potato salad and pickled celery. Don't skip the desserts (the strawberry and sorrel bread pudding with saffron ice cream is our favourite) or the well-thought-out drinks list, which includes cocktails made with fresh fruit. Landau and Jacoby's V Street (see p054) is also worth visiting for its vegan take on street food.
1221 Locust Street, T 215 320 7500, www.vedgerestaurant.com

Serpico

Chef Peter Serpico, a former honcho at New York's Momofuku, partnered with Stephen Starr to open this consistently lively eaterie on edgy South Street in 2013. The restaurant classifies itself as 'contemporary American', though the menu is more wide-reaching than that, featuring chilled dashi with cucumber, pea tendrils, crème fraîche and shiso; fried duck-leg sandwich with hoisin and pickle; and a lovely ravioli filled with a puree of dried sweetcorn, sourced from nearby Lancaster County. It's best to try a selection of dishes, and one of the 18 seats fronting the kitchen is an ideal place from which to do it. New York's Design Bureaux installed the charcoal-hued interiors and moody lighting. It's open for dinner only. *604 South Street, T 215 925 3001, www.serpicoonsouth.com*

Fitler Dining Room
Established in 2013 by Dan Clark and Ed
Hackett of nearby Pub & Kitchen (T 215
545 0350), popular with neighbourhood
gourmands, Fitler fits its area's laidback
bill nicely. The seasonal menu doesn't
break culinary ground, but classics, such
as Crab Louie salad with crumbled bacon,
and tender short ribs with gnocchi and
Swiss chard, are very well executed.
2201 Spruce Street, T 215 732 3331

Barclay Prime

When it opened in 2004, Stephen Starr's swish steakhouse was the talk of the town for its $100 Kobe beef, truffle and foie gras cheesesteak. Although the menu still has its gimmicks (like the $120 Wagyu version, served with a half bottle of Perrier-Jouët), they're not at all necessary: Barclay Prime can rest comfortably on its own merits. Starters of crab cakes, and beef tartare with dijon sauce, are consistent winners, the dry-aged ribeye is one of the best in Philly, and the macaroni cheese and tater tots (fried nuggets of grated potato) have cult followings. India Mahdavi melded her off-kilter, elegant style – of note here are the lime green, white and yellow leather armchairs – to the original features of the 1929 Barclay Building, formerly a hotel. *237 S 18th Street, T 215 732 7560, www.barclayprime.com*

Osteria

Seats at Marc Vetri's eponymous Spruce Street restaurant (T 215 732 3478) are among the most sought-after in the city, but his more casual venue, Osteria, is a perennial favourite too. Opened in 2007 in a former warehouse, the industrial, airy space with a red-stained concrete floor is a fine setting for Vetri's rustic Italian food. Osteria's pizza has earned the lion's share of the attention, and the Lombarda, with baked egg, Bitto cheese, mozzarella and cotechino sausage on a super-thin crust, certainly makes a great lunch if time happens to be tight. The wine list has 100 or so Italian labels to choose from, and the desserts are as good as the savoury dishes. Try the moreish polenta budino, topped with gianduia and candied nuts. *640 N Broad Street, T 215 763 0920, www.osteriaphilly.com*

Kensington Quarters

There's no doubt of the carnivorous focus at Kensington Quarters. You only just make it inside before coming across the mechanics of its adjoining butcher shop, which sets the tone well for this Fishtown restaurant/bar, opened by Jeniphur and Michael Pasquarello in 2014. Chef Damon Menapace sources free-range animals from local farms, and practises nose-to-tail cooking. Small plates such as BBQ chicken terrine are followed by a rotating selection of meaty offerings typified by the smoked sausage with spicy cabbage slaw and the KQ burger with organic cheddar in a house-baked brioche. Menapace also has a way with grilled vegetables. The interiors feature custom woodwork from Ben McBrien of Farmhaus (see p056). *1310 Frankford Avenue, T 267 314 5086, www.kensingtonquarters.com*

Mercato

Philadelphia does low-key neighbourhood restaurants very well, and there's often a queue for a seat at this BYOB set on a corner just off Avenue of the Arts. The 35-cover dining room is cosy rather than cramped, due to the warm colour scheme and exposed brick; it's a nice change from the starkness of some of the city's other BYOBs (there are many of these in Philly, and there's usually a charge for corkage).

Ryan McQuillan's seasonal menu merges classic and modern Italian cooking. The seafood and red meat dishes are especially good – try the spicy crab with squid ink bucatini; mussels and littleneck clams with sourdough; and balsamic-marinated skirt steak with a side of rosemary fingerling potatoes. Note that Mercato is cash only. *1216 Spruce Street, T 215 985 2962, www.mercatobyob.com*

La Colombe

Since it launched more than 20 years ago, La Colombe has been at the forefront of the city's burgeoning coffee-culture scene. This flagship, which opened in a Fishtown warehouse in 2014, was designed by local architects Stokes, and incorporates a bakery, café and roasting operation, as well as the distillery for Different Drum (overleaf), a coffee-infused sipping rum. Materials such as timber, brick and metal combine to enhance the industrial feel of the cavernous space, presided over by a large mural by New York artist ESPO. In addition to the house-made bread, there are salads, sandwiches and small dishes served in sizzling skillets. There's also, of course, plenty of joe – try the chilled draft latte, keg-poured for a frothy texture.
1335 Frankford Avenue, T 267 479 1600, www.lacolombe.com

High Street on Market

This artisanal bakery and casual café, the sister establishment to Ellen Yin's popular Fork (see p032) next door, has been a hit since it opened in 2013, thanks to chef Eli Kulp's approachable home-style cooking. The pastries are some of the best in town; try the savoury Red Eye Danish, filled with gravy, shaved Tennessee ham and Gruyère, while the pastrami on rye is the perfect snack for a walkabout. For dinner, the seasonal pasta dishes are a lesson in low-key sophistication – we suggest the caramelle with cauliflower, huitlacoche, rosemary oil and buttermilk. Local firm Marguerite Rodgers devised High Street on Market's pastoral-chic interior, which features wood cladding and church pew seating, anchored by the open kitchen. *308 Market Street, T 215 625 0988, www.highstreetonmarket.com*

Zavino

Chef Carlos Aparicio's Neapolitan-style slices and handmade pastas keep Zavino, a spacious, polished pizzeria, bustling. Try the Joey, topped with Berkshire pork sausage, mozzarella, provolone and spinach, or the delicate gnocchi served in a roasted cherry tomato sauce; the charcuterie and cheese list is also good. Interiors firm BoxWood has used rough-sawn timber and steel shelving to carve up the loft-like space into more intimate sections, and the combination of subway tiling, darkwood furnishings and parquetry sets a warm, industrial tone. Our favourite place to perch is at the Carrara marble bar that curves its way through the restaurant. Zavino's original branch (T 215 732 2400) is located on a Midtown Village corner. *3200 Chestnut Street, T 215 823 6897, www.zavino.com*

XIX

Situated on the 19th floor of the Bellevue, once known as the 'Grand Dame of Broad Street', café/bar/restaurant XIX shines for its French Renaissance-style interiors, which date to 1904. A 2006 renovation by Marguerite Rodgers enhanced the two circular dining spaces, featuring soaring domed ceilings and a huge chandelier. An all-day menu offers breakfast and lunch staples, and a fish- and seafood-centric dinner; try the sautéed Pennsylvania lake trout with Yukon Gold potatoes, or grilled Maine lobster. However, the real reason for visiting is the old-world bar (above), especially if you can secure a seat by the window for a superb skyline view. Despite the opulent surroundings, XIX is casual enough to be an impromptu cocktail stop. *200 S Broad Street, T 215 790 1919, www.nineteenrestaurant.com*

Girard

Once you adjust to the pop art-inspired interiors by Joshua Otto – seating in cobalt yellow and a ceiling dressed up in dazzle camouflage, a zebra-stripe pattern used to disguise WWI warships – you'll find out that Girard has much of what you want from your neighbourhood bistro, starting with a no-fuss menu of brasserie-style hits. Small plates include seasonal salads, pickled vegetables and pan-seared crab

cakes, while entrées and mains range from a burger with Gouda, bacon jam and duxelles to pork ribs glazed with bourbon and caramel, served with a broccoli slaw. Girard is BYOB – we suggest vodka to mix with the elderflower cordial or freshly squeezed lemonade. The optional tipping policy is unusual for an American eaterie. *300 E Girard Avenue, T 267 457 2486, www.girardongirard.com*

INSIDER'S GUIDE

BELA SHEHU, FASHION DESIGNER

A native of Albania, Bela Shehu moved to Philadelphia in 1997 and launched her clothing label, NINObrand (333 S 20th Street, T 267 761 9388; by appointment), which favours monochromatic hues, in 2002. She appreciates the city's warm attitude and slower pace, which she says 'makes it safe to experiment'. Shehu likes Joan Shepp (1811 Chestnut Street, T 215 735 2666) – 'a crown jewel' – for its progressive international labels, and also recommends Knit Wit (1729 Chestnut Street, T 215 564 4760), an eclectic womenswear boutique. For homewares, the bazaar-style Material Culture (4700 Wissahickon Avenue, T 215 849 8030) 'always tickles me'.

To relax, Shehu might take a dip in Devil's Pool, a swimming hole in Wissahickon Valley Park (www.fow.org), or indulge her sweet tooth at chocolatier Teuscher (200 S Broad Street, T 215 546 7600). She is a fan of V Street (126 S 19th Street, T 215 278 7943): 'Their dan dan noodles waken all dormant senses.' Shehu often visits homey Brick and Mortar (315 N 12th Street, T 215 923 1596) for an aperitif, before dinner at The Good King Tavern (614 S 7th Street, T 215 625 3700), for the French-inspired bistro menu, or laidback fine-diner Vernick (2031 Walnut Street, T 267 639 6644), housed in a Rittenhouse brownstone. Evenings might close with a nightcap at Ranstead Room (2013 Ranstead Street) or live music at the intimate Boot & Saddle (1131 S Broad Street, T 267 639 4528). *For full addresses, see Resources.*

ART AND DESIGN
GALLERIES, STUDIOS AND PUBLIC SPACES

Philadelphia has a storied artistic tradition – it's home to America's first-ever art school (see p064), and has also produced some of the best-known figures in the country's history, including Alexander Calder and Mary Cassatt. These days, the fact that the city often takes a back seat to the nearby creative mecca of New York doesn't mean that the local scene should be overlooked. It is energised and inclusive, and shot through with scrappy, do-it-yourself innovation.

You'll uncover this attitude in studios and hole-in-the-wall spaces. Head to the building that collective Vox Populi (see p063) shares with dozens of others, including Grizzly Grizzly (2nd floor, 319 N 11th Street). To the north, Kensington's former factories are being carved into co-ops, such as Little Berlin (2430 Coral Street), which support emerging artists. Established galleries congregate in Old City, as they have done for the past half-century, and there is a wealth of public sculpture (see p025), murals (see p070) and one-of-a-kind installations, not least the bizarre folk-art fantasy of the Magic Gardens (1020 South Street, T 215 733 0390).

This has always been a town of designers and makers, and work by a new wave of craftsmen is sold at American Street Showroom (see p058). Invest in young guns such as ceramicist Ian Anderson (opposite) and Ben McBrien (www.farmhausmodern.com), whose hardwood furniture melds midcentury lines with rustic charm. *For full addresses, see Resources.*

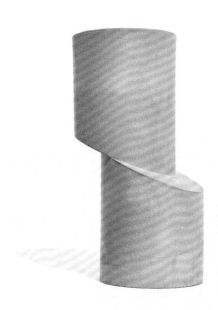

Aandersson

Fresh-faced Ian Anderson launched his line of sculptural ceramics in 2014. His work, produced at The Clay Studio (T 215 925 2453), has drawn attention for its conceptual yet functional form – the cast porcelain 'Oden' pitcher (above), $130, with its offset volumes, is case in point. Indeed, the city is proving to be a hothouse for talented potters. Felt+Fat (T 484 620 9272), a Port Richmond firm headed by Nathaniel Mell and Wynn Bauer, crafts tableware for many of the city's top restaurants, including Fork and High Street on Market (see p050). And Tyler Hays, whose design company BDDW has showrooms in New York and Milan, makes delicate mugs and limited-edition crockery using clay dug from a 20-foot hole behind his Philadelphia-based studio. *www.aanderssondesign.com*

American Street Showroom

Philadelphia's manufacturing sector was, for the most part, bust by the mid-1980s, and it nearly took Amuneal, a speciality metal fabricator since 1965, down with it. The founders' son, Adam Kamens, came on board in the early 1990s and revived the firm by shifting its focus to design-led custom metalwork. In 2013, he partnered with furniture-makers Groundwork and Robert True Ogden to establish American Street, turning an old electricity substation into a showroom. Craftsmanship is key, as seen in some of our favourite objects: handmade wooden chopping boards by Lostine, zinc tables with tree-stump bases by Groundwork, and Amuneal brass-and-oak shelving – clients include the Ace and Standard hotel groups. By appointment.
2201 N American Street,
www.americanstreetshowroom.com

Franklin Court

It comes as something of a surprise that a house of such historical significance as Benjamin Franklin's was razed. But indeed it was, in 1812, to make way for commercial development. Unable to adequately establish what a replica of his home and next-door print shop might have looked like, officials instead commissioned Robert Venturi's ghost structures – tubular steel outlines installed in 1976 above a subterranean museum dedicated to Franklin's life. The result is one of the most remarkable spaces in Old City. Venturi's svelte forms conjure the site's past without resorting to faux historicism, and make Franklin Court a lovely urban reprieve. Architects Quinn Evans added an elegant glass entry pavilion to the museum in 2013. *314-322 Market Street, T 215 965 2305*

Locks Gallery

Marian Locks opened this gallery in the back of a Rittenhouse store in 1968. It was one of the first local enterprises devoted to contemporary art and among just a handful of commercial outlets available to Philadelphia creatives. Today, Locks Gallery remains a key stop on the circuit, representing artists such as Bryan Hunt and Polly Apfelbaum, who showed 'Free Fall' (above) in 2015, as well as natives Elizabeth Osborne and the late Thomas Chimes. With an emphasis on painting and sculpture, its shows might not be bleeding edge but they're always very well curated. It is now housed in a 1920s palazzo-style building that sports an exquisite iron-gate entrance by master metalsmith Samuel Yellin. Closed Sundays and Mondays.
600 S Washington Square, T 215 629 1000, www.locksgallery.com

Vox Populi

By the late 1980s, the city was losing many up-and-coming artists to the 'Philadelphia Triangle', a term coined to explain the sudden disappearance of emerging talent, only for it to turn up again in a New York gallery. Vox Populi was founded in 1998 to reverse the trend. Operating as an artists' collective, it exhibits works by members, such as Erica Prince ('Dollhouse'; above), and invitees, as well as presenting guest-curated shows, films and workshops. A screening lounge and performance room supplement the four exhibition spaces. Vox is situated in an ex-factory complex, which also houses other galleries and studios, including the NAPOLEON group, meaning there's often engaging events going on. Closed Mondays and Tuesdays.
Third floor, 319 N 11th Street,
T 215 238 1236, www.voxpopuligallery.org

PAFA
The Pennsylvania Academy of the Fine
Arts, founded in 1805, has a permanent
collection of close to 14,000 pieces by
luminaries such as Georgia O'Keeffe and
Edward Hopper, housed in an exuberant
1876 Victorian Gothic pile. The school has
moved into an adjacent old car factory,
which offers further gallery space (work
by Traction Company; pictured).
1301 Cherry Street, T 215 972 2060

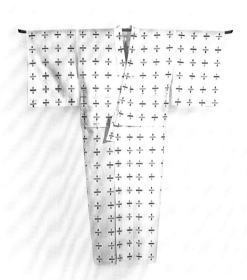

Fabric Workshop and Museum

Since its inception in 1977, this textiles workshop has drawn some of the top names in modern art — Howard Hodgkin, Anish Kapoor, Marina Abramović — to its residencies, thanks to the late founder Marion Boulton Stroud's vision for an environment of experimentation. It added 'Museum' to its name in 1996 to reflect the growing collection, which includes Chris Burden's *LAPD Uniforms* series. It now has a touring exhibition programme and publishing list, and is an outstanding contemporary art space. The 2015 show 'Both/And Richard Tuttle Print and Cloth' saw Tuttle, who has collaborated with FWM since the late 1970s, design *Extraordinary (W)*, a hand-sewn yukata (above), $2,000, which went on sale in the excellent shop. *1214 Arch Street, T 215 561 8888, www.fabricworkshopandmuseum.org*

Bahdeebahdu

Named after a dog that once lived in Old City (get the whole story when you visit), this studio/gallery, a partnership between interior designer RJ Thornburg and artist Warren Muller, is set in a former garage. You can't miss Muller's fantastical lighting sculptures and chandeliers, which he creates on site from found and salvaged objects, including farm equipment, car parts, musical instruments and cutlery.

They are large in scale and custom-made, and priced accordingly, from $2,700 to more than $25,000. Even if you aren't in the market, Bahdeebahdu is still worth browsing, and for the inside track on the local design scene. Check for exhibitions by local artists, such as Kevin Broad and David Matthews, in the gallery space.
1522 N American Street, T 215 627 5002, www.bahdeebahdu.com

Space 1026

Local artist collective Space 1026 has been producing edgy work out of its walk-up studio/gallery (ring the bell downstairs for entry) since it was founded in 1997. The high-ceilinged exhibition space displays pieces by emerging Philadelphian artists, such as Mat Tonellia, James John Small and Lynnea Holland-Weiss. Lisa Conn's 2015 multimedia show, 'The Better To Hold You With, My Dear' (above), featured a series of street-inspired paintings on 12 wood panels accompanying a marionette-style installation. There's also a small shop that stocks prints, books, films, T-shirts and 'zines, as well as works from past and current exhibitions. Most items are priced well under $50. There's an annual auction in December if you happen to be in town. *1026 Arch Street, T 215 574 7630, www.space1026.com*

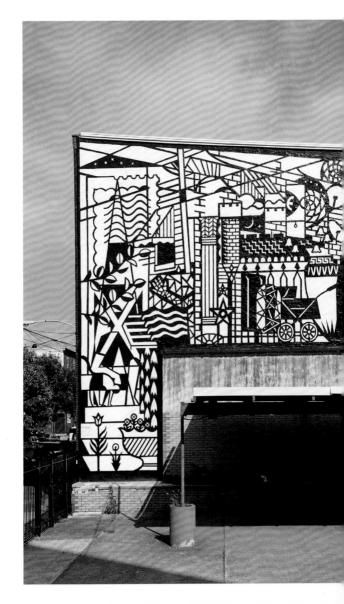

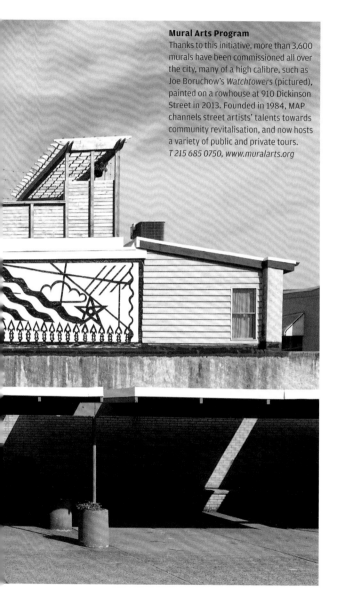

Mural Arts Program
Thanks to this initiative, more than 3,600 murals have been commissioned all over the city, many of a high calibre, such as Joe Boruchow's *Watchtowers* (pictured), painted on a rowhouse at 910 Dickinson Street in 2013. Founded in 1984, MAP channels street artists' talents towards community revitalisation, and now hosts a variety of public and private tours.
T 215 685 0750, www.muralarts.org

ARCHITOUR
A GUIDE TO PHILADELPHIA'S ICONIC BUILDINGS

From the red-brick austerity of colonialism to the glassy bravado of contemporary commerce, a great proportion of the history of US architecture is on display in Philadelphia. Though many leading practitioners were trained here throughout history, the cityscape remained traditional for years, punctuated by flashes of brilliance exemplified by Frank Furness and George Hewitt's Pennsylvania Academy of the Fine Arts (see p064), the 1932 PSFS Building (see p082), designed by George Howe and William Lescaze, and Frank Lloyd Wright's often overlooked 1959 Beth Sholom Synagogue (8231 Old York Road, T 215 887 1342), set in Montgomery Park.

Innovation began in earnest in the 1960s. Led by a group of visionaries that included Robert Venturi, Denise Scott Brown, Ian McHarg and Louis Kahn, the Philadelphia School moved past the modernist glass box into contextualism. Structures such as Kahn's Richards Medical Research Building (see p084) at the University of Pennsylvania, Robert Geddes' 1963 Police Headquarters (see p083) and Venturi's 1964 Vanna Venturi House, widely recognised as the world's first example of postmodernism, paved the way for fresh ideas and directions nationwide. Today, the city is once again full of energy and working to refine itself through new landmarks in the mould of Cesar Pelli's Cira Centre (see p010), and quietly impressive buildings such as Skirkanich Hall (see p078).
For full addresses, see Resources.

Barnes Foundation

The 2012 relocation of the art collection of Albert C Barnes is still a testy subject for some Philadelphians. The works were previously held on his suburban Merion estate and only rehoused after a long and public court battle that raged between the Barnes Foundation board and a citizens group that opposed the move. Architects Tod Williams Billie Tsien simply replicated the layout of the Merion galleries in Philly, with Barnes' treasures, including close to 180 Renoirs, hung just as they had been for nearly a century, yet the jury is still out on whether the soul of the institution has been lost. However, the building itself (overleaf), which is clad in offset Negev limestone panels, is self-assured and slots in comfortably amid public gardens.
2025 Benjamin Franklin Parkway,
T 215 278 7200, www.barnesfoundation.org

Barnes Foundation

Society Hill Towers

This group of three residential towers, completed in 1963 on the site of a former food market, was the zenith of a massive rehabilitation of Society Hill, one of the city's oldest areas. IM Pei designed the complex with his customary attention to detail. The buildings are positioned so that none blocks the others' views, and their carefully articulated concrete-and-glass facades reflect the geometry of the surrounding streets and the Federal and Georgian terraces that line them. The development remains a highly sought-after address more than 50 years on. If you don't happen to secure an invitation to one of the private residences, the next-best vantage point is the motor court, which features Leonard Baskin's sculptural set *Old Man, Young Man, The Future*.
S 2nd Street/Locust Street, T 215 923 4105

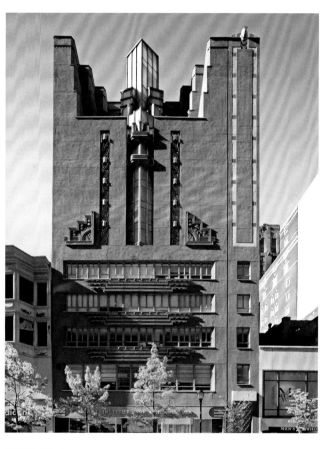

WCAU Building

The construction boom of the 1920s left Philadelphia with some accomplished art deco architecture, though nothing quite so flamboyant as the headquarters of the radio station WCAU, which was unveiled in all its glory in 1928. Architects Gabriel Roth and Harry Sternfeld studded the facade with reflective cobalt chips, surrounded the windows with zigzag panels of brass, copper and stainless steel, and topped it with an illuminated glazed tower bearing the company logo (the tower was later removed, but the WCAU lettering remains on the lift doors inside). A succession of renovations over the years have left little of the original interiors intact, although the current tenant, the Art Institute of Philadelphia (T 215 567 7080), carried out an exterior restoration in the early 1990s.
1622 Chestnut Street

Skirkanich Hall

Rather than deferring to the traditional red-brick architecture of the rest of the University of Pennsylvania campus, Tod Williams Billie Tsien shrouded the 2006 bioengineering faculty, Skirkanich Hall, in shingled glass, aluminium, zinc and glazed brick in a whole spectrum of shades from black to chartreuse. The combination is at once high-tech and organic, and melds beautifully with the early 20th-century buildings nearby, and KieranTimberlake's glassy Levine Hall to the west. Make sure to venture in to check out the five-storey atrium (opposite), where cherrywood and glazed yellow tiles, which reference the ginkgo trees outside, accent the granite finishes and exposed-concrete structure, which has been polished, sandblasted and hammered to suggest handworked stone. *210 S 33rd Street*

Singh Center for Nanotechnology
Weiss/Manfredi's 2013 research facility
for the University of Pennsylvania is airy
and inviting, unusual for a laboratory,
and scientists can be seen busy at work
through panels of orange-tinted, UV-
blocking glass. The signature feature is
a dramatic 21m cantilever, with views
over the campus, and the central quad
houses Tony Smith's *We Lost* sculpture.
3205 Walnut Street

PSFS Building

It seems a little odd that America's oldest savings bank would have built the world's most modern skyscraper as its HQ, but the Philadelphia Savings Fund Society did exactly that. Some 80 years on, this celebration of International Style appears as fresh as when it opened in 1932. Local architect George Howe and his Swiss-born associate, William Lescaze, conceived the 150m tower with sleek, contemporary lines and materials, including granite, marble, limestone and glazed brick, imported from 32 countries; the building cost $8m, which would have been an almost unimaginable figure during the Depression. Bower Lewis Thrower converted the office space into guest rooms and carried out a restoration of the public areas for its conversion into the Loews hotel (see p023) in 2000.
1200 Market Street

Philadelphia Police Headquarters

The Roundhouse, as locals call this police headquarters, doesn't always get the love it deserves. Philadelphians associate the building with past scandals, and officials complain that it is ill-suited to the needs of a modern force – it was inaugurated in 1963. That is a shame, because there is much to admire in the design. Architect Robert Geddes anchored the building with twin drum-shaped towers and wrapped it in a precast concrete skin. The result – a measured modernist structure with a sinuous form – is a blend of strength and grace, although the surrounding blank wall doesn't do it any favours. The police have announced plans to relocate to a new HQ in West Philadelphia in 2018, a move that may allow the Roundhouse to be appreciated with fresh eyes.
1 Franklin Square

Richards Medical Research Building
When the University of Pennsylvania commissioned Louis Kahn to design a high-rise laboratory in 1957, the architect had never worked on a high-rise or a lab. Kahn met the challenge, and influenced modern architecture in the process, by dividing the complex into its functional parts: the 'servant' and 'served', as he called them. Completed in 1965, five lab and classroom towers are grouped around two core buildings, containing mechanical and support systems; inside the towers, Kahn conceived column-free spaces made feasible by engineer August Komendant's pre-stressed concrete framework. Since then, tenants have subdivided the open-plan layout and blocked out the expanses of plate glass, as the scheme turned out to be not as practical as Kahn had hoped.
3700-3800 Hamilton Walk

30th Street Station
Chicago architects Graham, Anderson, Probst & White capitalised on this station's site, pointing its neoclassical columned portico towards the central skyline on the other bank of the Schuylkill. The massive proportions of the 1933 building are clear when you enter the stately main concourse (pictured), with its coffered ceiling, five-storey windows and art deco chandeliers.
N 30th Street/Market Street

SHOPS

THE BEST RETAIL THERAPY AND WHAT TO BUY

Unfortunately for Philadelphia, New York casts an inescapable retail shadow. But there's a lot to like here, and a host of inventive enterprises to track down. Center City shopping is focused on two neighbourhoods. There's a clutch of hip stores on N 2nd and N 3rd streets in Old City, including Sugarcube (124 N 3rd Street, T 215 238 0825), best for vintage pieces, and Meadowsweet Mercantile (see p092), a purveyor of carefully curated clothing, homewares and furniture. Rittenhouse Square has long been a destination for swankier establishments. Step off chain-saturated Walnut Street to seek out the jeweller Egan Day (see p094), as well as the off-beat gift emporium Stadler-Kahn (1724 Sansom Street, T 267 242 7154). Chestnut Street, once the main shopping drag, is on the rise again, due to Stars & Stripes (No 2129, T 215 587 2129), which specialises in heritage garments, Joan Shepp (see p054), Lapstone & Hammer (see p090) and Commonwealth Proper (opposite).

Midtown Village is a smaller but still more-than-worthwhile hot spot where you'll find boutique optician Modern Eye (145 S 13th Street, T 215 922 3300) and soap-makers Duross & Langel (117 S 13th Street, T 215 592 7627). Another area to watch is Fabric Row, situated off South Street; located here is jeweller Bario Neal (700 S 6th Street, T 215 454 2164), whose handmade rings are crafted from precious metals and ethically sourced soft-hued gems. *For full addresses, see Resources.*

Commonwealth Proper

Classic tailoring and modern sensibility intersect at this menswear store, situated in clubby rooms on increasingly smart Chestnut Street. Owner Craig Arthur von Schroeder founded the company in 2008 as an extension of his line of US-made ready-to-wear shirts, which it still offers, alongside a selection of ties, cufflinks, and pocket squares, but it is the bespoke shirts, suits, trousers and coats that are its bread and butter. The fabrics are top-notch – Vitale Barberis Canonico, Thomas Mason, Loro Piana – with sewing done stateside, mostly in Philadelphia and New York. The quick-drying, travel-friendly, Swiss-made Tech range is especially worth a look. Custom shirts start at $225, suits at $1,950, and will take six to eight weeks. *1839 Chestnut Street, T 267 319 1741, www.commonwealthproper.com*

Lapstone & Hammer

A slew of standout men's stores have opened in recent years, but none is quite as good-looking as Lapstone & Hammer, established in 2015. The interiors are by Kate Rohrer, who combined the sinuous curves of the existing art deco structure with polished walnut cabinetry by local furniture-maker Ben Johnson, and added midcentury leather sofas and custom-made orb lighting. It's an august setting for a well-edited range of streetwear, accessories and footwear, including Prps denim and plaid shirts, Garrett Leight sunglasses, Filling Pieces sneakers and Yuketen moccasin-style boots, crafted from Horween leather, as well as US-made grooming products, such as Beardbrand oils. A rotating selection of limited-edition and heritage trainers is displayed in a gallery-like space at the rear of the shop.
1106 Chestnut Street, T 215 592 9166, www.lapstoneandhammer.com

Meadowsweet Mercantile

Stacy Jackson opened this shop in 2011 with an emphasis on vintage items – a passion nurtured during weekends spent scouring flea markets as a child – paying heed to quality craftsmanship and utility. Thoughtful merchandising brings out the beauty in the found objects, be they a 1960s Scandinavian rattan toy rocker, a woven oak trapper's basket or vintage lace dresses. There is also a raft of items created by Philadelphia makers, including tunics by Lillian Jackson Textiles, a series of *yunomi* by potter Brian Croney, stylish ceramics by Felt+Fat (see p057), 'Bloak' hardwood ladders by Lostine (above left) and bags made from recycled leather and waxed canvas by Peg and Awl. The shelving was constructed by Jackson's husband and the minimal interiors are bright and airy.
47 N 2nd Street, T 215 756 4802

Sage

Philadelphia has long been a town of distillers – William Penn dabbled – and an enduring fondness for a tipple can be traced back to the American Revolution, when the city had one tavern for every 25 men. The tradition is continued by Art in the Age (see p028), which produces its own craft liquor range, with flavours steeped in US history. Sage (above), $32, takes its inspiration from Thomas Jefferson's garden – it has an herbaceous, woodsy aroma, and is best served on the rocks with mint leaves. We're also rather partial to Root, a heady, modern spin on the original, alcoholic 'root tea', a potent herbal brew popular in colonial times. It has notes of sarsaparilla and birch bark; pair with ginger beer. Each small-batch brew is made from organic ingredients. *www.artintheage.com/our-spirits*

Egan Day

Husband and wife team Kate Egan and Cort Day opened this store in a Victorian townhouse in 2008, offering handmade jewellery and objets d'art from a host of tricky-to-find designers. Everything here is exquisite, including the artful displays, which change daily. Look for Annette Ferdinandsen's nature-inspired earrings, gemstone pendants from Gabriella Kiss and angular silver and gold rings by local studio Editions De Re. Standout objects include BDDW hand-painted ceramic mugs (see p057), Ted Muehling's 'Biedermeier' candlesticks and Nymphenburg porcelain, as well as wall art by New Yorker Lindsey Adelman. Be warned, the knowledgeable staff will invariably point out something that you simply can't live without.
260 S 16th Street, T 267 773 8833, www.eganday.com

Norman Porter Company

Set in a former factory in Kensington, a neighbourhood that once hummed with manufacturing, Norman Porter Company has reintroduced quality craftsmanship and production to the area. Established in 2012 by brothers David and Michael Stampler, the firm launched with a line of no-frills, meticulously fashioned jeans, available in just two fits, each cut from American or Japanese selvedge denim in a workshop above the showroom. It now also produces trousers made from duck canvas, as well as leather tote bags and belts, cotton work aprons and T-shirts that are printed in Philadelphia. The studio oozes with industrial warmth thanks to its wood floors, leather armchairs and vintage sewing machines; visit by appointment.
150 Cecil B Moore Avenue, T 267 908 4694, www.normanporter.com

ESCAPES

WHERE TO GO IF YOU WANT TO LEAVE TOWN

Ask Philadelphians what they like best about their city, and one of the top answers will be how easy it is to leave. Of course, locals are not desperate to escape, but when they do, many of the best destinations in north-east USA are within easy reach. Directly to the west is Lancaster County, the home of the Pennsylvania Dutch (or Amish) community – a place that's full of rural charm and touristy schmaltz. Stop in the city of Lancaster to eat at Central Market (23 N Market Street, T 717 735 6890; open on Tuesdays, Fridays and Saturdays), the oldest farmers' market in the country, and if you decide to stay the night, try the Lancaster Arts Hotel (300 Harrisburg Avenue, T 717 299 3000). Further west of here is Pittsburgh, a city finding its post-industrial feet in its emerging areas and cultural attractions, notably the Andy Warhol Museum (opposite). Nearby, take advantage of a rare opportunity to rent out a Frank Lloyd Wright property, the 1957 Duncan House (187 Evergreen Lane, Acme, T 877 833 7829; brunch tours on Sunday).

And then there are two properly traditional getaways: the New Jersey shore to the south-east and the Pocono mountains to the north. The best hotels are the retro-cool Chelsea in Atlantic City (111 S Chelsea Avenue, T 800 548 3030) and the historic Fauchère in Milford (see p100) respectively. If you are travelling north, be sure to stop off en route at George Nakashima's studio (see p102). *For full addresses, see Resources.*

Andy Warhol Museum, Pittsburgh

Whenever asked where he grew up, Andy Warhol would reply, 'I came from nowhere.' 'Nowhere' was Pittsburgh, a gritty steel manufacturing centre about 500km west of Philly, where a young Warhol spent his days studying movie magazines at home and the altar in church – experiences that would shape his consumerism-as-religion pop art. The Andy Warhol Museum, which opened in a former warehouse in 1994, holds thousands of his paintings, drawings, sculptures and photographs, as well as an archive of his diaries and correspondence; it claims to be the most comprehensive single-artist collection in the world. Make the short drive to the excellent Carnegie Museum of Art (T 412 622 3131; overleaf), where Warhol took art classes as a child. *117 Sandusky Street, T 412 237 8300, www.warhol.org*

Carnegie Museum of Art, Pittsburgh

Hotel Fauchère, Milford

When Swiss chef Louis Fauchère bought a hotel in picturesque Milford in 1867, he set up both the town and surrounding Poconos as a getaway for the well-to-do. But the Fauchère closed in 1976, and the pretty Italianate building was left to deteriorate. Fortunately, locals Sean Strub and Richard Snyder recognised its potential, and reopened it in 2006 after a five-year restoration. New York-based designers Kureck Jones deftly combined a traditional look with modern touches; the 16 rooms feature Frette linens and heated bluestone bathroom floors. Dine in The Delmonico Room before having a nightcap in stylish Bar Louis. It is a two-hour drive to Milford, from where you can continue to the pristine beaches of Assateague Island. *401 Broad Street, T 570 409 1212, www.hotelfauchere.com*

George Nakashima complex, New Hope

About an hour north of Philadelphia is New Hope, where Japanese-American architect and furniture craftsman George Nakashima settled in 1943. His former home and studio complex, where his daughter Mira still produces work, was partly conceived by the designer. It is an experimental fusion of modernist and Japanese influences, as seen in the 1967 Arts Building (above). A plywood hyperbolic paraboloid shell forms the sweeping roof, and the exterior mural is by Ben Shahn. The compound is open to the public on Saturday afternoons and consultations for commissions can be booked by appointment. The Moderne Gallery (T 215 923 8536) in Philadelphia also sells a range of Nakashima's work. *1847 Aquetong Road, T 215 862 2272, www.nakashimawoodworker.com*

NOTES
SKETCHES AND MEMOS

RESOURCES
CITY GUIDE DIRECTORY

HOTELS

ADDRESSES AND ROOM RATES

AKA Rittenhouse Square 022
Room rates:
studio, from $180
135 S 18th Street
T 215 825 7000
www.stayaka.com

The Chelsea 096
Room rates:
double, from $250
111 S Chelsea Avenue
Atlantic City
T 800 548 3030
www.thechelsea-ac.com

Duncan House 096
Room rates:
house, from $425
Polymath Park
187 Evergreen Lane
Acme
T 877 833 7829
www.polymathpark.com

Hotel Fauchère 100
Room rates:
double, from $200
401 Broad Street
Milford
T 570 409 1212
www.hotelfauchere.com

Lancaster Arts Hotel 096
Room rates:
double, from $190
300 Harrisburg Avenue
Lancaster
T 717 299 3000
www.lancasterartshotel.com

Loews 023
Room rates:
double, from $200;
Luxury King, price on request
1200 Market Street
T 215 627 1200
www.loewshotels.com

The Logan 016
Room rates:
prices on request
1 Logan Square
T 215 963 1500
www.theloganhotel.com

Le Méridien 018
Room rates:
double, from $170;
Suite, from $270
1421 Arch Street
T 215 422 8200
www.starwoodhotels.com/lemeridien

Monaco 016
Room rates:
prices on request
433 Chestnut Street
T 215 925 2111
www.monaco-philadelphia.com

Hotel Palomar 017
Room rates:
double, from $190;
Presidential Suite, price on request
117 S 17th Street
T 215 563 5006
www.hotelpalomar-philadelphia.com

The Rittenhouse 029
  Room rates:
  double, from $250
  210 W Rittenhouse Square
  T 215 546 9000
  www.rittenhousehotel.com
The Ritz-Carlton 016
  Room rates:
  double, from $270
  10 S Broad Street
  T 215 523 8000
  www.ritzcarlton.com
Roost Midtown 020
  Room rates:
  studio, from $185
  (four-night minimum stay)
  111 S 15th Street
  T 267 737 9000
  www.myroost.com/midtown

WALLPAPER* CITY GUIDES

Executive Editor
Jeremy Case

Author
Jim Parsons

Art Editor
Eriko Shimazaki

Photography Editor
Elisa Merlo
Assistant Photography Editor
Nabil Butt

Sub-Editor
Belle Place

Editorial Assistant
Emilee Jane Tombs

Contributors
Julia Murphy
Clare Pelino
Danielle Sigel
Ann Tok

Interns
Chloe Lin
Daniella Shrier

Production Controller
Sophie Kullmann

Wallpaper*® is a
registered trademark
of Time Inc (UK)

First published 2010
Revised and updated
Second edition 2015

© Phaidon Press Limited

All prices and venue
information are correct at
time of going to press,
but are subject to change.

Original Design
Loran Stosskopf
Map Illustrator
Russell Bell

Contacts
wcg@phaidon.com
@wallpaperguides

More City Guides
www.phaidon.com/travel

Phaidon Press Limited
Regent's Wharf
All Saints Street
London N1 9PA

Phaidon Press Inc
65 Bleecker Street
New York, NY 10012

Phaidon® is a registered
trademark of Phaidon
Press Limited

www.phaidon.com

A CIP Catalogue record for
this book is available from
the British Library.

Printed in China

ISBN 978 0 7148 6852 3

PHOTOGRAPHERS

Cameron Blaylock
Fabric Museum and
Workshop, p067

Roger Casas
Philadelphia city view,
inside front cover
Cira Centre, pp010-011
Comcast Center, p012
City Hall, p013
Philadelphia Museum
of Art, pp014-015
AKA Rittenhouse
Square, p022
Art in the Age, p028
Barclay Prime, p042
Osteria, p043
Mercato, p046
XIX, p052
Bahdeebahdu, p068
Society Hill Towers, p076
WCAU Building, p077
Skirkanich Hall,
p078, p079
PSFS Building, p082
Philadelphia Police
Headquarters, p083
Richards Medical Research
Building, pp084-085
30th Street Station,
pp086-087

Joseph Hu
Locks Gallery, p062
Vox Populi, p063

Dutch Huff
Hotel Palomar, p017
Le Méridien, pp018-019
Loews, p023
Mark di Suvero sculpture,
p025
The Rittenhouse Spa &
Club, p029
Franklin Bar, pp030-031
Abe Fisher, p033
Dizengoff, pp034-035
Buena Onda, p036, p037
Vedge, p038
Serpico, p039
Fitler Dining Room,
pp040-041
Kensington Quarters,
p044, p045
La Colombe, p047,
pp048-049
High Street on Market,
p050
Zavino, p051
Girard, p053
Bela Shehu, p055
American Street
Showroom, p058, p059
Franklin Court, pp060-061
PAFA, pp064-065
Fabric Museum and
Workshop, p066

Space 1026, p069
Joe Boruchow mural,
pp070-071
Barnes Foundation, p073,
pp074-075
Singh Center for
Nanotechnology,
pp080-081
Commonwealth Proper,
p089
Lapstone & Hammer,
pp090-091
Meadowsweet Mercantile,
p092
Egan Day, p094
Norman Porter Company,
p095

Abby Warhola
Andy Warhol Museum,
p096

Matthew Williams
Roost Midtown, p020, p021

PHILADELPHIA
A COLOUR-CODED GUIDE TO THE HOT 'HOODS

UNIVERSITY CITY
Situated west of the Schuylkill, the student heartland is noted for its vibrant nightlife

SOUTH PHILADELPHIA
Check out the cafés and shops catering to a diverse population – Italian, Asian and Latino

FAIRMOUNT/ART MUSEUM
Tourists flock to the famous steps from *Rocky*, but seek out the spectacular river views

WASHINGTON SQUARE WEST
Catching up with the city's renewal, Wash West has hip bars and pretty residential streets

OLD CITY
Penn's waterfront stomping ground has cool shops and eateries amid the historic draws

CENTER CITY NORTH
Ignore the swarming suits; the business district also boasts markets and museums

RITTENHOUSE SQUARE
With upscale boutiques and the city's priciest properties, this is Philly at its most chichi

NORTHERN LIBERTIES/FISHTOWN
A prime example of recent gentrification, with ex-factories pulling in young bohemians

For a full description of each neighbourhood, see the Introduction.
Featured venues are colour-coded, according to the district in which they are located.